ROAD
Through the Ages

PHILIP STEELE

Illustrated by
ANDREW HOWAT and GORDON DAVIDSON

Troll Associates

Library of Congress Cataloging-in-Publication Data

Steele, Philip
    Road through the ages / by Philip Steele, illustrated by Andrew
Howat and Gordon Davidson
        p.   cm
    Summary: Surveys the history of roads and how they have changed
both the lives of humans and the face of the landscape over
thousands of years.
    ISBN 0-8167-2737-6 (lib. bdg.)   ISBN 0-8167-2738-4 (pbk.)
    1. Roads–History–Juvenile literature. [1. Roads–History.]
I. Howat, Andrew, ill.   II. Davidson, Gordon, ill.   III. Title.
TE148.S74   1993
625.7–dc20   91-35878

Published by Troll Associates
© 1994 Eagle Books

Design by James Marks

Printed in the U.S.A.

10 9 8 7 6 5 4 3 2 1

Introduction

This is the story of a road network and of the people who built it over the ages. You will not find the roads on any map, and they have never been given official numbers. However, there are many roads like them, and many that share their history.

This story is set in Western Europe, but roads were also built long ago in other parts of the world. The Royal Road of the Persians, in use from 3500 to 300 B.C., was more than 1,500 miles (2,400 kilometers) long. It was used by soldiers on the march. The road's surface was probably hard-packed soil, but one stone-surfaced section has survived in modern Turkey.

Fine roads were also built in ancient China. In 221 B.C. the Chinese emperor decreed that the roads used to carry the royal mail should be 50 paces wide. Five hundred years ago the Incas of South America also built long highways with tunnels, bridges, and causeways.

Today, major highways link cities around the world. In the United States alone there are more than 3,484,000 miles (5,607,000 kilometers) of surfaced road, used by more than 176 million motor vehicles.

Contents

Ancient tracks

The forest ran from the slopes of the mountains down to the windswept coast. The trees were dark and dense, and snow weighed heavily on the branches.

The landscape had not always looked like this. Long before humans existed, strange reptiles had roamed here and wallowed in steaming swamps. They had died out long ago.

By about 70,000 B.C., the climate had become bitterly cold. Ice covered the mountains. The forest was home to heavy-browed, hairy people who hunted bears and bison with crude stone weapons.

By 23,000 B.C. a broad track led to the caves on the ridge. The route was marked by the skull of a reindeer wedged into a tree trunk. This warned other tribes to stay away.

The first paths were of turf, twigs, or pebbles, beaten flat by galloping hooves and running feet. A network of paths grew up around the caves where the hunters lived. Short cuts were hacked out with tools of flint and bone.

By 35,000 B.C., Cro-Magnon people were living in the forest. We call them Cro-Magnon people after a cave in France where their remains have been found. They were clever hunters. The wild animals that lived in the forest beat their own paths through the undergrowth, and the hunters followed these ancient tracks.

New people arrive

Between 10,000 and 5000 B.C. the climate became much warmer. Soon forests of oak and ash were growing in the valleys. People learned how to grow crops and tame wild animals. New people arrived from the east bringing the secrets of working metal.

They fashioned tools of copper at first, and later learned how to mix copper with tin to make bronze. By 1400 B.C., villages had been built in clearings in the woods. Oxen hauled rough, wheeled carts along the muddy rutted tracks.

The skills of wheel making and horse riding had first been developed in distant Asian lands. Sturdy ponies were now used for long-distance travel. They followed the chalky, dry track that ran along the top of the ridge.

Who was using the ridgeway 3,400 years ago? Warriors came from distant lands. Merchants brought pottery, jewelry, and bronze knives to exchange for metals. Priests who worshiped the sun god used the track at midsummer. They visited the great stones that had been raised on the ridge 500 years before.

Celtic invaders

The years passed, and customs changed. The track along the chalky ridge between the mountains and the sea remained the chief route, or thoroughfare. It was used by invading armies and fleeing peasants.

8

The funeral processions of great chieftains passed along its route. In times of peace, sheep were herded along the road, and creaking ox carts carried freshly cut hay.

Celtic invaders built a great fortress on the ridge in 200 B.C. A ramp led steeply downward through a series of banks and ditches, with layers of timber and boulders for support. On fine mornings in winter the royal charioteer would thunder down, wheels spinning. Sometimes the young nobles of the tribe would race each other for fun and bet on the result.

The iron-rimmed chariot wheels were designed for the battlefield, not for narrow paths or rough ground. Travelers bound for the forest or the mountains rode small, sturdy ponies or went on foot.

The Celts were skilled metalworkers in gold, bronze, and iron. Their chariots were made of wood and metal. The warrior stood behind the driver and dismounted for hand-to-hand fighting.

Roman road

The Roman legions invaded by sea in A.D. 50. Rank upon rank of Roman soldiers battled with the Celtic warriors. The fortress was burned down and a military camp erected. This soon became a large town.

Heavy loads were carried by ox cart, while mules and horses hauled light carts. Most people still traveled on horseback, except for the soldiers of the legions. They marched until they were exhausted, counting the milestones erected along their route.

The Romans were great engineers. Their roads ran straight and true for hundreds of miles. Some were over 39 feet (12 meters) wide. By the year 200 it was possible to travel far and wide.

Army surveyors decided to build the road straight through the oak forest. Soldiers burned down groves of trees that had been Celtic holy places, and cleared areas surrounding the road to prevent ambushes.

The base of the road was rocks embedded in sand. Layers of gravel and cement were laid over this. The surface was made of close-fitting stone blocks. It was slightly arched, or cambered, so water drained away.

11

The route of flight

In the year 410 the legions withdrew to Rome, which was being attacked by fierce warriors from the east. A few retired soldiers stayed behind and banded together with the Celts to defend the region against newly arrived invaders.

For hundreds of years there was hunger and war. The Roman town was burned and occupied by savage strangers. The old Roman road was no longer safe for travelers. The overgrown roadside hid robbers and cutthroats. Fortunately, there were inns where weary travelers could stay. Rooms were crowded, but there was a blazing fire, food and drink, and a song or story from a wandering poet.

The road itself became cracked, and weeds grew between the paving stones. However, it had been so well built that it survived, and parts of it can still be seen today. No better road was built in the region until the 1800s.

12

In the year 600 traveling on the old Roman road was often dangerous. In times of war, the ancient tracks through the forest became crowded with refugees— farmers, merchants, and priests.

Even in times of peace, travel by road was difficult. Most people chose not to travel at all.

The Middle Ages

The Normans invaded the region in the 11th century. They built a rough-and-ready castle of wood on the slopes of the ridge. By the year 1375 this had been replaced by a massive stone building surrounded by defensive walls.

A fine city grew up beside the castle, and this too was surrounded by thick walls. The road into the city passed through large gates, which were closed at night. The streets inside were narrow and muddy, because there was no proper drainage. There were many slippery alleys with steep steps. Outside the walls there were orchards and fields of vegetables.

The old Roman road led to a gate of the city. A thousand years of winter frost and summer dust had worn the road down, and in places it was badly rutted. The Christian pilgrims who flocked to worship at the great cathedral often approached the city on the ancient ridgeway, stopping to pray at shrines along the way.

The lord of the castle was a harsh master. However hard the peasants worked, they seemed to get nothing. At harvest time wagons loaded with grain creaked along the road, but it had to be ground into flour at the lord's mill. Neither the king nor the lord of the castle built new roads. When they went hunting in the forest, they rode along muddy tracks and splashed through streams. Sometimes they were ambushed by outlaws banished from the city.

15

The royal carriage

The city prospered. Woolen cloth, woven from the sheep that grazed the ridge, was shipped overseas. Some of the new merchants were now richer than lords, and the old castle lay in ruins. The richest family of all lived outside the city. They cleared part of the forest to make a deer park and built a splendid palace on the hill. One day in the spring of 1580, a royal messenger galloped to their door. The queen herself would be visiting the region in a month's time and wished to stay with them.

The country people had never seen a carriage and thought it was grand. In reality, it was very uncomfortable. It had no springs, and no glass in the windows. The Royal Progress was slow, as the state of the roads was poorer than ever. However, the queen insisted she needed to make sure that her subjects were loyal.

When the queen arrived, she was in a bad mood. So were her attendants and her escort of soldiers. It had been raining for weeks, and the road was deep with mud. The royal carriage had been stuck at the crossroads for hours. Farm boys and servants from the inn had placed brushwood under the wheels, and they heaved and shoved until the carriage was free. One of the horses had lost a shoe, and there had been a further delay at the blacksmith's shop.

17

Post haste!

One fine morning in 1675 a man stood outside the city, making a drawing. He carefully measured the roads and inked them in like ribbons across the paper. He drew in hills, windmills, church spires, and other landmarks. The map was to be printed for travelers.

The roads were busier than ever. Mail boys galloped from one town to the next with saddlebags full of important packets and letters. They blew a horn to warn everybody that they were on official business and in a hurry.

In the city, there were coaches for hire. Some rich people complained that so much traffic was breaking up the road. However, they often sold their old carriages to public operators.

Coaches were now a common sight, and some even had glass windows and steel springs. They needed them. The road was as bumpy as ever, dusty in summer, and icy in winter. Each village and town was supposed to repair the roads, but many failed in their duty. In some places travelers now had to pay to use the roads. These fees, called tolls, were collected at gates called turnpikes. The tolls were supposed to pay for the road repairs.

19

The highwayman

Dusk fell early in December. The highwayman edged into the shadow of a tree and quieted his restless horse. He pulled out a flintlock pistol, poured gunpowder into the priming pan, and snapped back the cover. It was beginning to snow.

Soon his horse pricked up its ears. There was a distant clatter of hooves and the sound of a trumpet. The stagecoach was approaching.

The stagecoach guard was nervous, because his coach was carrying rich passengers. The road down from the ridgeway was lonely and these were lawless times. The guard gripped his wide-barreled musket called a blunderbuss.

The highwayman galloped from the shadows. The horses reared and the coach lurched. There were screams. The guard saw a white face and blasted the shadowy form with his blunderbuss. The highwayman fired wide, his arm broken and bleeding. The stagecoach rushed on to the city and safety.

By 1750 stagecoaches were carrying mail and passengers from one city to another. The armed guard and the driver sat outside, while the passengers jolted along inside the cab. The journey often took many days. The coach stopped each night at an inn. The horses were changed at each stage of the journey.

21

New engineered roads

This was an age of engineering. Huge gangs of workmen dug canals to link cities across the country. Other workers were building a new railroad.

New roads were built, too — the best since the days of the Romans. They were used by light, horse-drawn carriages, which could travel quickly without lurching over bumps or becoming stuck in the mud.

Modern roads were first built in the 1760s by the French engineer Pierre-Marie Trésaguet. He laid layers of small stones over strong stone foundations. The Scottish engineers Thomas Telford and John McAdam used carefully graded stones and gravel to build fine roads in Britain during the 1820s. By 1835 a long road had been built inland to replace the old Roman road.

The construction of new roads was paid for by tolls. Rich travelers could afford to pay the tolls, but local farmers were often too poor to pay for each cartload of hay that passed through the tollgate. They cursed the new roads!

Bicycles and cars

During the 19th century, many of the main roads around the city were improved using the McAdam method. Chips of broken stone laid over the surface were pressed down by the weight of traffic, forming a waterproof surface. It was found that the seal was improved if the stone base was filled with asphalt tar. Treated surfaces were called "tarmacadam" or "tarmac" roads. Country lanes remained unsurfaced, or "unmetaled."

By 1905, better road surfaces had

Air-filled tires were developed for bicycles in 1888 and used on cars in 1895. They made the ride smoother, but stones and loose horseshoe nails caused many punctures. Driving in 1905 was far from comfortable. Cars often broke down, and there were few garages to fix them. Drivers and passengers sometimes wore scarves and goggles to protect their faces from the dust.

become necessary. New vehicles were taking travelers far from the city. Bicycles had become very popular by the 1890s, and the first modern motorcycle, with an engine between the wheels, had been built in 1901.

Horses took fright when these early vehicles chugged by. The first successful gasoline-powered car had been built in Germany in 1885. In 1905 both gasoline- and steam-driven cars were seen on the road.

The growth of road travel

The first cars were expensive, but during the 1920s driving became cheaper. People could now live outside the city, and take a bus, car, or train into work each day. City dwellers could travel out to the country on weekends.

By 1935 the city was spreading outward, and more and more roads were built to outlying areas and suburbs. The busiest route was expanded into a four-lane roadway. This carried two lanes of traffic in each direction, separated by a central barrier.

Many roads were now surfaced with tarmac or concrete paving. They had to be repaired frequently as traffic became heavier. Some busy intersections were controlled by automatic traffic lights, which had been invented in the United States in the early 1920s.

By 1935 motor traffic had changed many streets. Cars were now parked along the roadside. There were garages and filling stations.

As cars became faster, police had to make sure that drivers drove slowly through towns and that vehicles were safe.

The present

The city grew and grew, and its streets filled with traffic. In 1960 a new superhighway was built that followed the route of the old Roman road. The first superhighways were built in the 1930s in Germany.

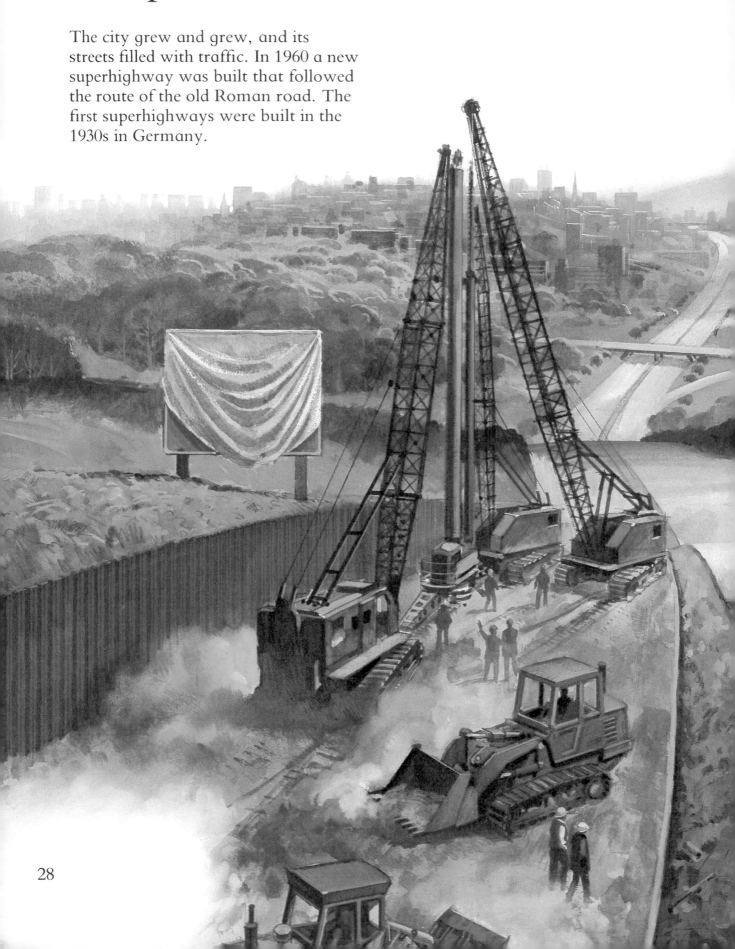

Superhighways were designed for speed and safety. There were no intersections, traffic lights, or parking.

Large signs and warning signals helped direct the traffic. The road was leveled and covered with gravel, which was then compacted. This was overlaid with concrete, strengthened by a mesh of steel bars.

In 1990 work began on a new road that would circle the city. During the excavation of the ridgeway section, a bulldozer uncovered some ancient remains. Archaeologists said they belonged to Cro-Magnon hunters.

The future

The Cro-Magnon hunters would have been amazed at the roads of the future. They had not known the wheel or the carriage, let alone the automobile, bus, or truck—just a few of the many inventions since prehistoric times.

However, during the 1990s some people began to question the value of those inventions. Superhighways and city streets were jammed with traffic.

Exhaust fumes created a dense smog above the city. People began to plan new transportation systems that were cleaner and less wasteful.

The road has gone through many changes over the years. But it still helps us get where we want to go.

In this city of the future, private cars are banned. Public transportation run by electricity takes people to and from work. Railroad lines and canals are fully used, and bicycling is a popular pastime once again. The power of the sun is harnessed by solar cells, which provide lighting for the streets at night.

Index